Spanning Centuries

Spanning Centuries

The Remarkable True Legend of Martin's Mill
Bridge (and the Community Who Saved Her)

Kirsten Hubbard

Sponsored by Ken and Bonnie Shockey

Better Humans Books

This book would not be possible without the generous support of:

Ken and Bonnie Shockey

FRANKLIN COUNTY | PA

Great moments along the way.

ExploreFranklinCountyPA.com

Allison-Antrim Museum, Inc.
Ken and Bonnie Shockey
Cheryl Walburn, Parks Director
Chris Ardinger, Antrim Township Administrator

Antrim Township Supervisors
Fred Young III, Chairman
Pat Heraty, Vice Chairman
John Alleman, Member
Chad Murray, Member
Rick Baer, Member

Parks Committee
Cheryl Walburn, Parks Director
Thom Moore, Chairman
Jason Reiber, Vice Chairman
Andrew Barbuzanes, Member
Nate Bacon, Member
Natalie Schiro, Member

Ghost Writer LLC
Jesse McCleary, Editor
Christiana Martin, Editor
Tawny Gallagher, Editor
Abigail McElhiney, Graphic Designer

Carved in Time

"EGM 1888"
"D I HAYES 1901"
"HEM 1953"
"ME 1957"
"Steven & Penny 76–79"

Etchings still grace Martin's Mill Bridge

Folks in these parts have been marrying their stories to this old covered bridge for at least seven generations. By the measures of kin, that would be your great-grandmother's great-grandmother's mother. They carved their initials, maybe a date or a name if it were short enough. Sweetest perhaps are those lovers' hearts etched on the woven trusses that shielded kisses from the censure of a stricter time.

There's no malice in the act of these carvings, nothing as intentional as vandalism. Mind you, don't you go carving on that bridge. Treat it like a memorial of a kind, respectful of those who forged this place and then preserved it. More it seems that "HEM" and "Steven & Penny" sought an eternal connection to this mystical place, where trees cool the summer heat and the sound of wooden planks surf the river and echo soft and rhythmic as you ride or run or bike over them. So much so, you turn at the end and go back the other way just to hear the lullaby. It seems those old etchers believed the bridge could carry them long after they themselves had crossed from this world. And, so far, they were right. This bridge has a touch of immortality to it—it has survived the worst nature and politics and war and man's neglect could conjure and that rightfully should have destroyed it.

Yet it stands, and it remembers "HEM" and "HAYES" and the awkward, tender heart of "Steven & Penny." It holds a whole lot of stories, even more than those etched in its bones. Hewn on these pages are just a few of the most well-known. If you long for more stories, the ones that whisper just under written history and textbooks and genealogy records, then settle for a spell on the banks of the ancient creek and watch the shadows of stonework dance the tide and listen to the breeze. Those old trees are apt to rustle out a few more tales.

Bridging Our Past

The story of Martin's Mill Bridge begins with those who walked and loved and worshipped and died along the banks of the Conococheague millennia before us. They whose knowing of this land eclipses ours tenfold. The Susquehannok, Shawnee, Lenni Lanape, and Delaware tribes hunted, fished, and foraged these fertile forests, meadows, and tributaries.

These first inhabitants bestowed the fitting name Conococheague on the creek that ebbs and flows below Martin's Mill Bridge. The name itself, meaning "many-turn-river," speaks to an intimate relationship with the waterway. The 53-mile-long creek originates in South Mountain, flows southwest from its origin point, turns west at Caledonia, continues into the Great Appalachian Valley, turns southwest, and flows west again before emptying into the Potomac River about 20 miles south of the bridge.

Our modern macadam roadways are built on the Native Americans' innate knowledge of this valley's geography. Martin's Mill and its namesake bridge owe their location to the countless steps of original inhabitants who forged pathways of least resistance over thousands of years.

To learn more about the indigenous tribes of the region, visit Allison-Antrim Museum, highlighted in the Visitors Section in the back of this book.

European settlers first arrived in the late 1730s or early 1740s. David and John Kennedy took up a homestead near the point where the east and west branch of the creek meet. William and James Cross neighbored the Kennedys with a large farm. Both enjoyed and benefited from cordial relations with their Native American neighbors. By 1769, tensions were mounting between the natives and settlers, with the Cross settlement then referred to as "Cross's Fort."

A Lancaster man by the name of Jacob Graff recorded a deed on the Cross property in 1785, and this is where we find the first reference to a grist mill and saw mill. The mills were located just south of what is now the western entrance of the bridge.

In 1786, Dr. Robert Johnston, an Antrim Township native and Revolutionary War surgeon, purchased the land and built an estate just south of Greencastle. According to a 1798 tax document, the property included a 40'x40' stone grist mill, a saw mill, a 74'x28' barn, and a 25'x18' log house on 210 acres. The mills are listed as "Peter Righter's grist and saw mill." Interestingly, Dr. Johnson would host George Washington, who was a close friend and personal client, at his estate while the general marched toward the Whiskey Rebellion.

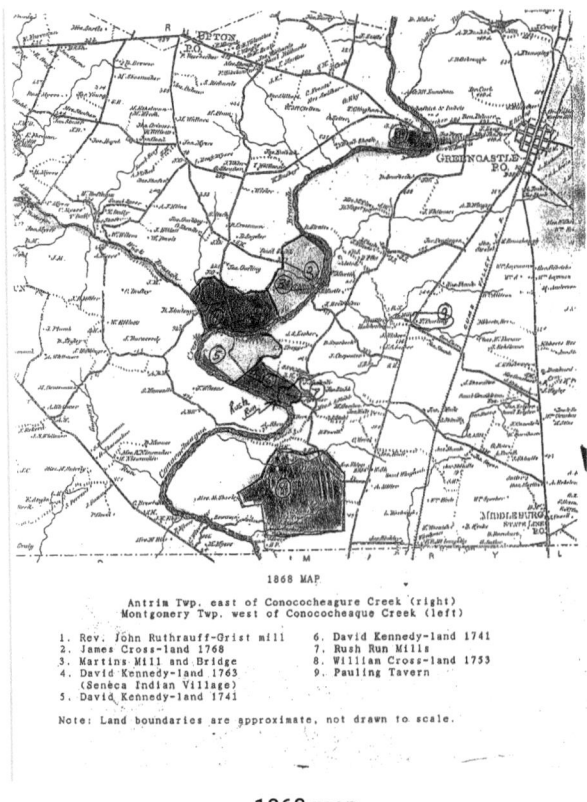

1868 MAP

Antrim Twp. east of Conococheague Creek (right)
Montgomery Twp. west of Conococheaque Creek (left)

1. Rev. John Ruthrauff-Grist mill
2. James Cross-land 1768
3. Martins Mill and Bridge
4. David Kennedy-land 1763
   (Seneca Indian Village)
5. David Kennedy-land 1741
6. David Kennedy-land 1741
7. Rush Run Mills
8. William Cross-land 1753
9. Pauling Tavern

Note: Land boundaries are approximate, not drawn to scale.

1868 map

1849—The Origin Story

It was January 19, 1849, when Antrim and Montgomery Township citizens asked the Franklin County commissioners to consider erecting a crossing at the mills.

The year 1849 was a time of great movement and technological innovation. The Civil War wouldn't erupt for more than a decade. James Polk, presiding over an America that had but 30 states, became the first sitting president to have his photograph taken. Austria conducted the very first air raid in world history during a battle against Venice by employing a pilotless balloon. Locally, residents found their collective voice as *The Conococheague Herald*, now *The Echo-Pilot*, began publishing a weekly newspaper. And rumor had spread by 1849 that gold was plentiful in California, spurring the Gold Rush, along with an interest and investment in mass transportation.

Both Antrim and Montgomery townships, along with their citizens, supported the appeal for a bridge. The creek formed the border between the two municipalities until 1872, when Montgomery became a part of Antrim. A bridge at the mill would replace an old low-lying ford that frequently flooded, was in disrepair, and was often impassable. The bridge would provide safe and reliable foot, horse, and carriage transport, easing supply and delivery routes and connecting the townships, as well as the Cumberland Valley and Maryland.

The commissioners agreed to approve and help fund the project, and a call for proposals was released.

Martin's Mill - date unknown

The Innovation of Bridges

Women walking from Martin's Mill Bridge - circa 1890s
Courtesy of Allison-Antrim Museum, Inc.

"Most people think of bridges merely as parts of the scenery. They forgot that the bridge is among man's earliest and most important inventions – one, like the wheel, which determined his future history...By enabling man to surmount a water barrier it permitted him to explore, colonize, and conquer. It influenced the location of towns and cities, led to creation of states and empires, and facilitated the spread of civilization."—G. Fred Ziegler, The Martin's Mill Covered Bridge, Prepared for Rededication of the Bridge on June 2, 1973

If one doubts humans' continued reliance on bridges, one need only look to the recent collapse of Baltimore's Francis Scott Key Bridge. In addition to the human loss are regional and nationwide economic burdens related to commerce, supply chains, tourism, and commuting.

In 1849, a bridge at the mill was an investment in economic development, a sign of rural progress and movement. The winning proposal was that of Jacob Shirk, who resided in the vicinity of the mills. Shirk proposed a 205' bridge built in the then-popular Town's lattice truss style. Patented in 1820 by Ithiel Town, this style gained popularity because it was cheaper and more easily constructed and adapted than traditional arch-support bridges.

The crisscross pattern of the wooden trusses, pinned with trunnels, was strong enough for a 200' span that could withstand horse and carriage traffic without exterior supports or arches. As the ford at Martin's Mill was 205', Shirk added a stone support at the bridge's midway.

While chosen for economics and practicality, the aesthetics of the Town truss design lent a uniquely endearing charm. The latticework resembles a woven basket, cocooning one in a soothing pattern of solid timber that feels safe and cozy—surrounding one with nature's strength and man's ingenuity. Sunlight and moonlight alike sneak into the small rectangular windows, shadowboxing from the lattice to the planks. Bookending the structure are large formal entryways that create a striking sight from inside the long, dark corridor. One cannot help but reflect upon the metaphor "a light at the end of the tunnel." The exterior of the tunnel was painted barn red with a black roof, blending with and reflecting the style of the mills and neighboring farmsteads.

Several of the workers, those who carried the wood and placed the pegs and made the final cuts, took to carving their initials in the trusses. If you spend some time tracing the past in the timbers, you can still find their engravings.

So it was that in early 1850, a new red covered bridge began carrying people, horses, and buggies across the Conococheague, also carrying the carvings of the craftsman who built her into the new century.

Early Bridge Life

Sitting as it did along a winding rural road and picturesque creek, the bridge quickly captured the hearts of locals. There were ample grassy banks along the creekside for picnics, gradual slopes into shallow waters for dipping toes or watering horses, and trees that cooled the summer heat far before air conditioning was commonplace. The bridge offered travelers a respite during rains and sheltered lovers from prying eyes.

The bridge also served its original purpose: providing safe and reliable passage across the Conococheague, connecting the mill to supply-and-demand routes and connecting the two townships.

The latticework design bore pedestrians, horses, and wagons for decades. Perhaps due to its remote location, the bridge survived the Civil War when many other bridges were burned. Entering the new century, its sturdy foundation could even withstand the weight of America's newest obsession—the automobile. Even as the mills were torn down in the early 1900s, the bridge continued to serve the township. But by the 1920s, the prevalence of automobile travel and the advent of heavier trucks began to strain the structure designed for the weight of horse-drawn carriages. By 1928, wear and tear on the bridge necessitated the first major restoration.

Automobiles crossed the bridge meant for horse and carriage.

Less than a decade later, the devastating flood of 1936, caused by copious amounts of rapidly melting snow and ice, inflicted major damage throughout Pennsylvania. Entire towns flooded, bridges were wrecked, and at least ten people lost their lives. Shindle's Bridge, as it was then called for the family residing in the nearby farmhouse, survived again, though not without scars.

In the 1940s, a truck crashed inside the bridge, causing damage to the flooring that required repair. Yet still the bridge stood. In the 1950s, weight limits were imposed, and the bridge's value and relevance began to be called into question.

Drama in the Courtroom

In 1958, the bridge was closed by the Franklin County commissioners under the recommendation of the county surveyor. The commissioners deemed the bridge hazardous and unnecessary, with repair or replacement causing undue burden on the county and its taxpayers. The overtone was that Shindle's Bridge would be abandoned and razed. The story was important enough to make front-page news on *The Echo-Pilot*, which shares a birthday with the bridge.

The Echo-Pilot, along with local residents, rallied to protect the beloved trestle and lead a grassroots protest. Editorials pointed to the recent closing of a second local bridge and suggested that the combined closings of the two bridges would set residents back to the pioneer age of "fords and ferries." A petition was circulated challenging the commissioners' classification of Shindle's Bridge as "unnecessary." One hundred and forty two signatories vowed they regularly utilized the bridge. In response to the petition, the commissioners delayed a decision on the future of the bridge, though the bridge remained closed until the matter underwent further review.

At the next commissioners' meeting, and to the ire of petition signers, the commissioners stood by their original decision to condemn the bridge. One commissioner added fuel to the protest by publicly stating that he believed 80–90% of the petition's signers did not, in fact, regularly use the bridge but had signed the petition in friendship of those few who did. That statement heightened tension and gave fodder to the inevitable court hearing.

That hearing began in June. About 40 people crowded the courtroom of Judge Depuy. Twenty-nine residents testified in defense of the bridge, making several courthouse trips for the elongated trial at a time when traveling to Chambersburg was still an occasion.

Drama infused the proceedings from the beginning when, in the opening statements and among increased press coverage and more widespread interest, the opposition recalled the commissioner's statement referring to the citizen petition signers he was elected to serve as "liars."

Bridge supporters argued the bridge was still necessary, that repair or replacement was not burdensome given county spending on other bridges, and that the commissioners lacked authority to close the bridge. No mention was made at the time regarding the historic or cultural contributions of the bridge or the surrounding area's recreational and scenic value.

After the first day of the hearing, Judge Depuy delayed further testimony so he could visit the bridge himself.

Reading like a courtroom thriller, during the trial an Antrim Township supervisor testified for the county, and the county treasurer and a U.S. mailman testified for the opposition, which caused party divisions and affected politics in Franklin County and personal lives for generations.

In the end, and almost reluctantly, Judge Depuy sided with the commissioners, stating that the county taxpayers should not be held accountable for an expense that benefited so few residents. Even so, he laid the expense of the court proceedings on the county rather than the opposition and earnestly praised the opposition for their civic engagement. But the result was that the commissioners could abandon and raze the bridge at their leisure.

There is a very old and very wise saying that winning comes in many forms, and here that is true.

With elections now just months away, the bridge had become a formidable political issue, gaining supporters, including the Covered Bridge Association, and press coverage far beyond Franklin County. In this political landscape, the commissioners had apparently lost their appetite to destroy the bridge. Though they had fought hard to gain the legal right to do so, they failed to take action or give orders to raze the bridge.

In November, all three commissioners were ousted. The new commissioners, perhaps learning from their predecessors, were more friendly to preserving the beloved bridge that was now formally recognized by its current name.

Martin's Mill Bridge had weathered what few do—a political storm. Under the protection of its neighbors, the bridge survived to span the next decade.

Martin's Mill Bridge Association

With the community, press, voters, and newly elected commissioners on their side, bridge supporters began creating an association to care for the bridge.

With assistance from the Covered Bridge Association, Martin's Mill Bridge Association was formed for the sole purpose of caring for the iconic bridge. Incorporators were Olin L. Hess, Nora J. Hess, Paul E. Garling, William O. Shuman, Paul L. Witmer, and Robert W. Barnhart. Joining the incorporators on the first board of directors were Maynard Statler, Greencastle-Antrim planning board; Robert H. Cordell, secretary, Antrim Township supervisors; Benjamin Thomas, president, Greencastle Coach Company; and G. Warner Harsh, executive vice president, Citizens National Bank of Greencastle.

On October 8, 1962, Judge Depuy, the same judge who sided with the then-commissioners to condemn the bridge, rescinded his own order and transferred ownership to the new Martin's Mill Bridge Association.

– SPECIAL RECOGNITION –

Mr. and Mrs. Hess, former residents of Antrim Township, donated the land northeast of the bridge for use as a public park and picnic area. They also donated land on both sides and under the bridge and leased additional ground, southeast of the bridge site, to the Association. For many years Mr. Hess served as President of the Association and helped maintain the grounds. We extend our sincere appreciation to Mr. and Mrs. Hess for their contributions.

MR. AND MRS. OLIN HESS

From The Martin's Mill Covered Bridge, Prepared for Rededication of the Bridge on June 2, 1973

That same year, Olin and Nora Hess donated six acres of easement and parkland along the east of the bridge to the newly formed association. The association raised $4,000 and enlisted dozens of volunteers to widen access roads, create a turnaround, clear land for a formal picnic area, and combat vandalism.

In September 1965, seven years after it was condemned, though it remained closed to traffic, the bridge was rededicated, along with the new park.

Most Beautiful Bridge in the World

Three years later, the devotion and persistence of the supporters were rewarded as Martin's Mill Bridge gained international recognition. The span was named one of the twelve most beautiful spots in the world by Trans World Airlines, with a full-color photo appearing in the airway's 1968 calendar. But another challenge was just on the horizon.

Agnes!

The worst storm in national history at the time hit U.S. shores with a vengeance in mid-June 1972. Pennsylvania would take the brunt. Hurricane Agnes slammed the Caribbean before shattering the U.S. coastline in Florida, Georgia, and South Carolina. In North Carolina, the gale restrengthened before arcing into the Atlantic Ocean and circling back to mainland America's northeast. The flooding in Pennsylvania was epic. Of the 128 deaths attributed to Agnes, 50 were Pennsylvanians. Agnes remains the wettest tropical cyclone on record in the state. Some towns were under 13' of water, the governor and his wife had to be evacuated via boat, campers were rescued by helicopters, and thousands were trapped in their homes. Three thousand businesses and 68,000 homes were demolished, causing $2.3 billion in destruction. Over 220,000 Pennsylvanians were left homeless. One hundred and fifty bridges across the Commonwealth were rendered impassable or swept away. Martin's Mill Bridge was one of them.

Agnes leaves Martin's Mill Bridge shattered
Glen Myers

The entire 205' structure was upheaved from its stone foundation by a swollen, angry river and smashed into the trees on the banks of the creek. In the wake of the devastation, many of those 150 destroyed bridges were abandoned. Looking at the carnage of Martin's Mill Bridge, one might assume it would suffer the same fate.

But one would fail to take into account the determined community that had already saved the beloved bridge from floods, car wrecks, and politicians.

The bridge lay battered on the banks of the creek, with broken trusses and shattered lumber littering the creek and banks. So violent was the storm that splintered wood even reached the treetops. But the members of Martin's Mill Bridge Association talked in terms of restoration rather than demolition, hiring Chambersburg engineering firm Nassaux-Hemsley to assess the damage.

The engineering report outlined the complexities of restoration: trusses would need to be painstakingly numbered, and the shattered bones of the bridge would need to be carefully lifted from their current precarious positions, disassembled on safe ground, and reassembled using the numbered markings as a guide. Replacement planks, trusses, and pegs for those pieces missing or beyond repair would need to be custom fabricated.

Stones from a nearby abandoned arch bridge would form a foundation from which the reconstructed bridge would be raised four feet to protect it from future flooding.

Reconstruction would be an enormous challenge—a massive puzzle requiring herculean effort, specialized skills and equipment, massive volunteer hours, money, the goodwill of the community, and the political backing of the township and county. But, yes, it was possible.

The association approved the plan with one caveat: reconstruction should prioritize saving the carvings. Where possible, the words whittled in the timber over half a century ago should be placed as such to be visible to passersby.

Reconstruction commenced in fall 1972, with a full community effort. Nassaux-Hemsley led the engineering. Robert W. Barnhart, one of the founders of Martin's Mill Bridge Association, acted as foreman.

Local company Grove Manufacturing, now Manitowoc Crane, provided cranes. The 377th Engineer Battalion of Chambersburg, the 357th Transportation Company, and the National Guard donated equipment and labor.

Cranes begin meticulous reconstruction
Glen Myers

Corning Glass Works contributed $1,500. William O. Shuman organized dozens of volunteers and raised over $8,000. Reginald Miller Sons leveled the ground. Bonded Applicators donated paint. Craftsman Dean Heinbaugh masterfully led the masonry of stone arches. Valley Transit Mix supplied concrete. Myers and Fitz, Maugansville Lumber, Armco Steel Co., and Harmon Musselman donated materials or provided deep discounts.

The Borough of Greencastle and Antrim Township loaned equipment and labor. Antrim Township supplied infill, widened the road, and managed water runoff. Greencastle-Antrim High School's woodshop class fabricated 1,600 wooden pegs.

Residents donated shale, paint, and equipment. Civic clubs, scouts, church groups, families, and individuals came in droves to volunteer on weekends, cleaning debris, sawing, nailing, numbering, masoning, and measuring. Dixie Motel and Restaurant fed the volunteers. Each person gave what they could to save the bridge and preserve the old carvings.

Martin's Mill Bridge was rededicated in 1973

On June 3, 1973, after eight months of cleaning, dismantling, erecting piers, fundraising, reassembling, and painting, Martin's Mill Bridge was rededicated and opened for traffic for the first time since 1958. The following year, the bridge was enshrined into the National Register of Historic Places.

"HEM" and "Steven & Penny" were now national treasures.

The Five

The community had once again saved their beloved bridge, and their meticulous work held for decades. But the decision to reopen the bridge to traffic came at a cost. By 1986, a state-mandated review once again deemed the structure unsafe and ordered the bridge closed.

The weight of daily use had worn the bridge that was never designed for automobile traffic. The floor planks in the middle had become distorted. A large hump had formed at the point where the planks met the stone pier that had been added in 1973 to raise the bridge above flood levels. Planks at both entrances were rotting from exposure to snow and rain, and the entire bridge leaned precipitously over its base.

Tension cables were used to straighten the bridge's frame

Tension cables were added to the bridge's frame in an attempt to realign it to its foundation. By 1991, it was clear the solution was not working, and the bridge's condition further deteriorated. The midway hump had worsened, plank rot had exacerbated, the roof leaked, exterior paint peeled, and vandalism was frequent.

The plan for repairing the structural deficiencies started with lowering the midway stone support and inserting wide wood buffers between the stone pier and the bridge's planks, thus distributing weight more evenly. The bridge's dangerous lean would be fixed by inserting steel support frames, then bracing the original trusses to that support frame.

Estimates for repairing the bridge were difficult to obtain. The complex project was outside the capabilities of some local businesses. Several firms declined submitting proposals because they felt more substantial interventions—a complete reconstruction or replacement—were needed. But, with little money and a complete reconstruction anticipated to cost hundreds of thousands of dollars, Martin's Mill Bridge Association had little choice but to pursue less intrusive and less costly repairs.

At last, the association found a company that would take on the challenging structural repairs. The cost would be just over $33,000, with a timeline for completion by 1999, just in time for the bridge's 150th anniversary.

With no money, but great faith in a community that had rescued the iconic bridge time and time again, the association approved the plan pending funding. Their faith was not displaced.

The fundraising effort included auctions, dinners, coin buckets, and house tours; appeals to businesses, banks, and residents; and requests to foundations and the Commonwealth. Volunteers committed to doing some repairs, lessening the cost. By 1993, enough funding was secured to begin the project. Community support didn't stop there.

While the project relied on the generosity of many, five volunteers worked the project as if it were their calling: Al Bonnell, Mike Mess, Bruce Moats, Frank Larson, and Gene Snider.

These five labored at least every Tuesday, prompting the nickname the Tuesday Bridge Club. They replaced rotting planks, sanded vandalism, scraped and repainted the bridge's barn-red clapboard siding, realigned eight windows, and completely replaced the entire 20' roof and its underlayment. The work was long, difficult, and sometimes daunting. They painstakingly replaced and painted siding on 20' scaffolding erected on wagons anchored in the creek. With the work complete, The Five put the finishing touches on the bridge, with a wooden sign that still graces the eastern entrance.

Generous donations for the restoration of the bridge: Top: John Buchanan and Glenn Hykes accepting an $18,000 State Initiative Grant check from Rep. Pat Fleagle. Center: Glenn Hykes and John Shubert accepting an award and $1500 donation from Franklin County Heritage Inc. Bottom: Polly Beers with a few of the birdhouses which she decorated with hand painted flowers that were sold at the Preservation Auction.

Fundraisers contributed significantly to the reconstruction

Scaffolding was erected on wagons anchored in the creek

Within just three years, four years ahead of schedule, the bridge was rededicated as a part of Greencastle's Old Home Week. As if The Five's contributions were not impressive enough, they also built a miniature Martin's Mill Bridge float for the Old Home Week parade!

Martin's Mill Bridge Association had once again triumphed over what seemed impossible odds to salvage the bridge from ruin to glory —for now. Even before the last peg was set in this most recent gallant effort, the question loomed: What about next time? How would the association raise funding for the next major renovation, one that might easily exceed a million dollars? What would happen when the next devastating storm or flood ripped across the Conococheague? The Five knew intimately the work involved to repair the bridge. Could they stake the future of the revered historic landmark on the assumption that another Five with the skills, time, and will would materialize when the bridge needed it?

The rising expenses, insurance, and fundraising needed to care for the aging bridge eclipsed what a small group of even the most devoted citizens could realistically provide. Martin's Mill Bridge Association had done its job—carried the bridge from being condemned to being celebrated as a national treasure. With love for the bridge and respect for those memorialized in its timbers, the association began searching for ways to protect the cherished icon long-term and ensure the resources needed to span another 150 years.

The Five replaced the entire roof and its underlayment

Siding was replaced and painted

A hump in the midway required repair

The Township Rises

In 2003, Martin's Mill Bridge Association transferred the bridge and the parkland to Antrim Township. Antrim Township already owned 138 acres of parkland that abutted the bridge and its property. Marrying the two parcels would amplify park services to the community while supporting the long-term preservation needs of the historic structure. To ensure local residents continued to have voice and agency in decision-making with regard to the bridge, the structure and adjacent park came under the purview of the community-led Parks Committee.

The wisdom and foresight of the Martin's Mill Bridge Association in transferring owner-ship of the structure and property was evidenced in the following decades. As predicted by the volunteers who knew her best, by 2015 Martin's Mill Bridge required a complex reconstruction that was estimated at $1.1 million.

The 2015 renovation reinforced the original wood structure

Antrim Township tapped its resources as a municipality to se-cure $245,00 in federal funding with the help of Rep. Bill Shuster and another $700,000 from the Federal Highway Administration Covered Bridge Preservation Fund. With additional funding committed by the township's landfill/park fund, the bridge was shored by more extensive steel supports; siding was added; and the roof, which had been a victim of vandalism, was once again replaced.

The Town's truss style is recreated during the 2015 renovation

The original wood structure was reinforced with steel

175 Years Later

Today, Martin's Mill Bridge and Martin's Mill Bridge Park combine with Antrim Community Park to produce a cohesive park system while retaining their unique recreational assets. Antrim Community Park now offers over 225 acres of sports fields, playgrounds, hiking and biking trails, parking, dog parks, pavilions, and restrooms in a serene setting among meadows, forests, and a pond. Martin's Mill Bridge Park adds a creekside picnic, grilling, and playground area; access to fishing, kayaking, and other water sports; and connection by road and trail to Antrim Community Park.

Thanks to a community that would allow neither nature nor politics nor time nor apathy to defeat her, the barn-red covered bridge still perches upon the banks of the Conococheague. She is both modest and proud, both scarred and perfect. Time has tucked her into the slopes of the greenery, softened her into the landscape. She is older than most of the trees that surround her, hewn from their grandfather's timber. And still she carries the chiseled hopes of our ancestors, who believed she held a touch of immortality. So far, they are right.

Martin's Mill Bridge dressed for winter

Present for the Future

Following a planning process that included extensive public input, Antrim Township released its Municipal Parks Master Plan in fall 2023.

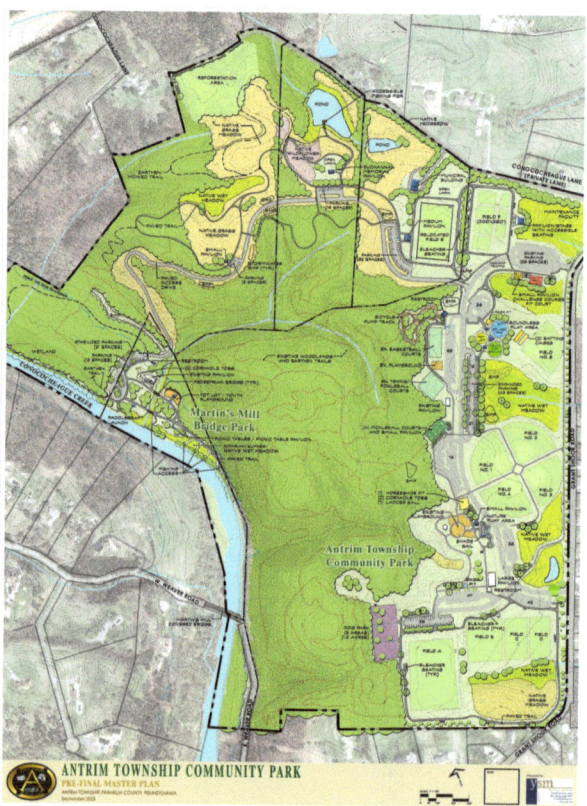

2023 Antrim Township Master Plan

In relation to the bridge and its park, the Master Plan prioritizes safety, accessibility, and conservation efforts.

The most significant improvement will be mitigating long-standing safety issues on the approach to the bridge. The current steep and winding roadway creates hazards to modern traffic and pedestrians. Sharp curves make it difficult to navigate or see oncoming traffic, and there are no guardrails to prevent cars from careening off precipitous cliffs.

Where the roadway levels at the bottom of the hill, it is prone to abrupt flash flooding. The nature and geographic features of the free-flowing Conococheague Creek mean that on a sunny day the creek can carry unexpected and swift flooding from storms far upstream. Flash flooding at the low point of the road, with no other egress, isolates the park area, leaving visitors trapped.

Emergency services are called several times per year due to these conditions.

To mitigate these dangers, the 2023 Municipal Park Master Plan proposes a new access road—the Martin's Mill Bridge Park Access Road—on recently acquired parkland. The road will traverse the east side of Antrim Township Community Park and enter Martin's Mill Bridge Park to the north, where the landscape is more gently graded and flooding to the south of the park will not block entry and egress.

Thoughtful in design, Martin's Mill Bridge Park Access Road provides benefits beyond mitigating urgent visitor safety. The new road will:

- double as a hiking, walking, and biking trail through serene meadows and forests, land that was previously inaccessible.
- give access to a pond with an ADA fishing pier solely for use by youth, veterans, and those with disabilities.
- connect and maximize other efforts and investments in both parks, including upgrades at Martin's Mill Bridge Park, acquisition of the newly acquired acres, fishing ponds, and ADA enhancements throughout both parks.

Upon completion of the proposed access road, the current road will be repurposed as a walking and biking trail. The current road will also remain an access point for township or emergency vehicles.

The new road will eradicate vehicle traffic passing directly by Martin's Mill Bridge, protecting the historic asset by reducing pollution and deterring vandalism.

Additional investments at Martin's Mill Bridge Park will include increased accessibility with ADA picnic tables, benches, and trash cans; enhanced creek access with an upgraded ADA paddle craft landing and additional fishing points; and fortified creek frontage with native plants to expand the riparian buffer to protect the watershed.

Antrim Township invites you to etch your mark on the bridge in several ways:

- Visit! Park hours are posted by scanning the QR code below or visiting twp.antrim.pa.us/parks-and-recreation/martins-mill-bridge-park.
- Get involved! Volunteers have been the heart of the bridge for 175 years. Individuals and groups can volunteer for various maintenance and improvement projects or sit on committees.
- Learn! Learn more about Martin's Mill Bridge and the history of our community by visiting our Visitors Guide partners.

Scan here to visit the Antrim Township Parks and
Recreation Department

Allison-Antrim Museum, Inc.
365 S. Ridge Avenue, Greencastle, PA 17225
greencastlemuseum.org

Ebbert Spring Archaeological Preserve and Heritage Park
12633 Molly Pitcher Highway, Greencastle, PA 17225
greencastlemuseum.org/ebbert-spring-park

Conococheague Institute
12995 Bain Road, Mercersburg, PA 17236
cimlg.org

Franklin County Visitors Center
15 South Main Street, Chambersburg, PA 17201
explorefranklincountypa.com

Enoch Brown Memorial Park
2730 Enoch Brown Road
Greencastle, PA 17225
twp.antrim.pa.us/parks-and-recreation

Greencastle-Antrim Chamber of Commerce
217 East Baltimore Street
Greencastle, PA 17225
greencastlepachamber.org

Jerome King Playground
240 North Carlisle Street
Greencastle, PA 17225
jeromekingplayground.com

Witherspoon Covered Bridge
Mercersburg SE Anderson Road
Montgomery Township, PA 17236